S.H.I.F.T.

Powerful Planner & Journal

FOR AN UNAPOLOGETICALLY KICK-ASS LIFE

Dr. Dara

The author and publisher have taken reasonable precautions in the preparation of this book. However, neither the author nor the publisher assumes any responsibility for any errors or omissions. The author and publisher specifically disclaim any liability resulting from the use or application of the information contained in this book, and the information is not intended to serve as legal, financial, psychological, or other professional advice related to individual situations. The advice and strategies in this book may not be suitable for every situation, and neither the author nor the publisher are held responsible for the results accrued from the advice and strategies in this book.

© 2022 Dr. Dara DeLeon. All rights reserved.

No part of this book may be reproduced, stored in a retrieval system, or transmitted by any means, electronic, mechanical, photocopying, recording, or otherwise, without written permission from the publisher. If you purchase this book without a cover, you should be aware that this book may have been stolen property and reported as "unsold and destroyed" to the publisher. In such case, neither the author nor the publisher has received any payment for this "stripped book."

Published by Drend Publishing

For ordering information or special discounts for bulk purchases as well as booking Dr. Dara to speak or host an event, visit DrDara.com.

Cover and Interior Design by Kim Baker / Orange Brain Studio
Editing by Lesley Marlo / ExpertCopy

ISBN: 978-0-578-32839-3

S.H.I.F.T.

FOR AN UNAPOLOGETICALLY
KICK-ASS LIFE

This planner & journal
for an unapologetic kick-ass life belongs to:

_____

_____

How will I SHIFT this year?
I believe in the value of a personal mission statement to make daily choices and remind me of what really matters to get my SHIFT together.

My mission statement for a kick-ass life:

_____

_____

_____

_____

"

To heal is to...
To have clarity and peace.
To feel happy and content
and peaceful.
To experience complete self-
acceptance.
To have authentic connection
and meaningful relationships
with others.

Dr. Dara

"

Dear you,

It is time to get real. I mean really, really real. Time to stop shoulding on yourself and "Get Your S.H.I.F.T. Together!"

What does this mean? Maybe you are suffering in some way – your relationship isn't giving you any love, your job sucks, your family makes you wish you were switched at birth...

If this sounds familiar, you my dear are stuck in the middle wishing you had something, were something, felt something different but plodding along in a mediocre, substandard, not-living-up-to-your-potential existence.

When you are stuck in the middle, you do things you don't really want to do. You make foolish decisions or hide in a shell, not taking risks or living life. You see yourself as not enough or inferior. You settle, you placate, you apologize for your existence.

UNTIL NOW!

If somewhere inside you feels the tiniest desire to have more, do more, be more, live more, and you are willing to open to the possibility that "YOUR" life can be a life that lights you up making you happy to be alive? Then you are ready to Get Your S.H.I.F.T. together.

With your S.H.I.F.T. together, you will meet your inner Superhero, unmute the internal Rockstar, own your magnificence, and watch your relationships, job, bank accounts, and family dynamics miraculously transform.

If you are ready to look in the rearview mirror of your life and see the skid marks you left on your road to bliss, stop waiting to start the ignition, and floor the gas!

Warmly,

Dr. Dara

Your No Bull-S.H.I.F.T., Mental fitness, Advice giving, Shame Abolishing, Health Advocate and Doer

It's time to get your

S.H.I.F.T.

together

S.H.I.F.T. Explained

Spirituality
Identify what makes you feel connected at a deeper level
(religious services, nature, yoga, meditation, time alone, etc...)

Health
Fill your love cup with a realistic schedule, exercise, rest, and food
(fitness schedule, sleep/rest schedule, nutrition plan, medical appts., self-care, etc.)

Interpersonal
Establish your needs with family and friends
(dates with your partner, time with friends, quality communication, etc...)

Finance
Determine your budget and financial goals
(income, savings/debt reduction plans, investment goals, etc.)

Trade
Know what you want in your career/daily task mastering
(schedule, environment, roles, goals, etc...)

How to use this planner
TO GET YOUR S.H.I.F.T. TOGETHER

3 STEPS TO GET YOU THERE:

1. Dumping the To-Don'ts

Consider what did not work for you or what you no longer want from the previous year or month. List what you want to dump in the To-Don't column as it comes up and at the end of each month.

2. Change your To-Dos into Ta-Dahs

Think about what is working, what did work, and what you want more of in life. Under Ta-Dahs, list what you are grateful for. Giving energy to what you want more of creates true fulfillment, breaking you free from the prison of "need-tos" and "to-dos."

3. Fuel your S.H.I.F.T.

Set your goals, your dreams, and your visions into 5 categories: Spirituality, Health, Interpersonal, Finance, and Trade

Tips for Success

- Be as specific and detailed as possible when setting your S.H.I.F.T. goals.

- Place your S.H.I.F.T. priorities on the calendar first and add the rest of your commitments around it.

- On the lined pages, jot down your thoughts and journal your uninhibited mind.

- Each day, write the steps you are taking to keep your S.H.I.F.T. together.

- Instead of using phrases like "I need" or "I want" replace with "I get to."

- Feelings fade unless re-stimulated. When journaling, don't re-read it. If it is important or requires follow up, circle it.

- In the beginning of each week, write the actions of your S.H.I.F.T. as if they have already happened. At the start of each week, write the outcome of your S.H.I.F.T. as if it has already happened. E.g. This week, I feel..., I see..., I hear..., I know...

- If you miss a day, a week, or a month, start writing whenever you remember.

- Don't feel like writing? Do it anyway. Write whatever comes to mind and don't judge. Progress is stronger than perfection.

- It's O.K. to have the same S.H.I.F.T. goals every month. Repetition reinforces the affirmation.

INTRODUCING YOUR NEW BEST FRIEND
THE F*CK IT BUCKET

{ If you get stuck, feel overwhelmed, can't decipher your feelings, or can't figure out what to do next..... **PUT IT IN THE F*CK IT BUCKET!** }

What is THE F*CK IT BUCKET?

Think of the **F*CK IT BUCKET** like a sand pail with a shell strainer at the top. When you put shells in the bucket, the sand, gunk, and dirt falls through to the bottom. The ick sifts off, and eventually you're left with only the treasures.

After you toss your issues, "stuckness," and uncertainty in the bucket, the **SH*T** falls away and the valuable stuff stays at the top.

Apply this to the stickiest, most annoying decisions you "have to make."

Take the dilemma, put it in the **BUCKET**, and do nothing with it for 24 hours. If you can't let it marinate for **24 hours**, at least give it a few hours.

If you have to decide how you feel about something or determine something in less time than that — the answer is **NO!** Because WHAT THE HELL is so much more important that you have to know RIGHT now?

After putting it in the **F*CK IT BUCKET**, what you thought was important will no longer have energy or power. Life choices will find you with certainty, ease, and excitement.

Calendar
2022

January
Su	Mo	Tu	We	Th	Fr	Sa
						1
2	3	4	5	6	7	8
9	10	11	12	13	14	15
16	17	18	19	20	21	22
23	24	25	26	27	28	29
30	31					

February
Su	Mo	Tu	We	Th	Fr	Sa
		1	2	3	4	5
6	7	8	9	10	11	12
13	14	15	16	17	18	19
20	21	22	23	24	25	26
27	28					

March
Su	Mo	Tu	We	Th	Fr	Sa
		1	2	3	4	5
6	7	8	9	10	11	12
13	14	15	16	17	18	19
20	21	22	23	24	25	26
27	28	29	30	31		

April
Su	Mo	Tu	We	Th	Fr	Sa
					1	2
3	4	5	6	7	8	9
10	11	12	13	14	15	16
17	18	19	20	21	22	23
24	25	26	27	28	29	30

May
Su	Mo	Tu	We	Th	Fr	Sa
1	2	3	4	5	6	7
8	9	10	11	12	13	14
15	16	17	18	19	20	21
22	23	24	25	26	27	28
29	30	31				

June
Su	Mo	Tu	We	Th	Fr	Sa
			1	2	3	4
5	6	7	8	9	10	11
12	13	14	15	16	17	18
19	20	21	22	23	24	25
26	27	28	29	30		

July
Su	Mo	Tu	We	Th	Fr	Sa
					1	2
3	4	5	6	7	8	9
10	11	12	13	14	15	16
17	18	19	20	21	22	23
24	25	26	27	28	29	30
31						

August
Su	Mo	Tu	We	Th	Fr	Sa
	1	2	3	4	5	6
7	8	9	10	11	12	13
14	15	16	17	18	19	20
21	22	23	24	25	26	27
28	29	30	31			

September
Su	Mo	Tu	We	Th	Fr	Sa
				1	2	3
4	5	6	7	8	9	10
11	12	13	14	15	16	17
18	19	20	21	22	23	24
25	26	27	28	29	30	

October
Su	Mo	Tu	We	Th	Fr	Sa
						1
2	3	4	5	6	7	8
9	10	11	12	13	14	15
16	17	18	19	20	21	22
23	24	25	26	27	28	29
30	31					

November
Su	Mo	Tu	We	Th	Fr	Sa
		1	2	3	4	5
6	7	8	9	10	11	12
13	14	15	16	17	18	19
20	21	22	23	24	25	26
27	28	29	30			

December
Su	Mo	Tu	We	Th	Fr	Sa
				1	2	3
4	5	6	7	8	9	10
11	12	13	14	15	16	17
18	19	20	21	22	23	24
25	26	27	28	29	30	31

To-DON'TS

Write down any past stuff that's not welcome in your future.

_____
_____
_____
_____
_____
_____
_____

Ta-DAHS

List what is working, what did work, and what you want more of in your future.

_____
_____
_____
_____
_____
_____
_____
_____

Spirituality

Envision and write your monthly goals towards your yearly **S.H.I.F.T.**

Envision and write your monthly goals towards your yearly S.H.I.F.T.

Interpersonal

Envision and write your monthly goals towards your yearly **S.H.I.F.T.**

Finance

Envision and write your monthly goals towards your yearly **S.H.I.F.T.**

Envision and write your monthly goals towards your yearly S.H.I.F.T.

_____
_____
_____
_____
_____
_____
_____
_____
_____
_____
_____
_____
_____
_____
_____
_____
_____
_____
_____
_____

> Today, I chose the path of love. I invite love on my journey. I choose loving actions. I am love.
>
> —Dr. Dara

Notes

Month _____

Sunday	Monday	Tuesday	Wednesday

20 ———

Thursday	Friday	Saturday

To-DON'TS

Write down any past stuff that's not welcome in your future.

_____
_____
_____
_____
_____
_____
_____

Ta-DAHS

List what is working, what did work, and what you want more of in your future.

_____
_____
_____
_____
_____
_____
_____

Notes

Spirituality

My monthly spiritual **S.**H.I.F.T. goals

_____
_____
_____
_____
_____
_____
_____
_____
_____
_____
_____
_____
_____
_____
_____
_____
_____
_____

I connect with nature when...
_____
_____

Spirituality

I am...

Peaceful

Health

My monthly health S.**H**.I.F.T. goals

_____
_____
_____
_____
_____
_____
_____
_____
_____
_____
_____
_____
_____
_____
_____
_____

To fill my love cup: Food, exercise, and rest looks like…

_____
_____

Health

Food · Rest · Exercise

S M T W T F S	nutrition	hours slept	activity	duration
○ ○ ○ ○ ○ ○ ○				
○ ○ ○ ○ ○ ○ ○				
○ ○ ○ ○ ○ ○ ○				
○ ○ ○ ○ ○ ○ ○				
○ ○ ○ ○ ○ ○ ○				
○ ○ ○ ○ ○ ○ ○				
○ ○ ○ ○ ○ ○ ○				
○ ○ ○ ○ ○ ○ ○				
○ ○ ○ ○ ○ ○ ○				
○ ○ ○ ○ ○ ○ ○				
○ ○ ○ ○ ○ ○ ○				
○ ○ ○ ○ ○ ○ ○				
○ ○ ○ ○ ○ ○ ○				
○ ○ ○ ○ ○ ○ ○				
○ ○ ○ ○ ○ ○ ○				

healthy meal ideas: _____
_____

self-care appointments this month: _____
_____

medical appointments this month: _____
_____

Interpersonal

My monthly interpersonal S.H.**I**.F.T. goals

_____
_____
_____
_____
_____
_____
_____
_____
_____
_____
_____
_____
_____
_____

I will spend time with...
_____
_____

Interpersonal

Goals for this month

Finance

My monthly finance
S.H.I.**F**.T. goals

_____
_____
_____
_____
_____
_____
_____
_____
_____
_____
_____
_____
_____
_____
_____
_____

Financial independence looks like...
_____
_____

Finance

Finance ∴ Budget ∴ Savings

Income

Date	Service	Amount

Savings

Date	Deposit	Paid Date	Balance

Monthly

Total Income	
Total Budget	
Total Savings	
Total Expenses	

$$ Goals:

Debt

Due	Bank	Amount Paid	Balance

Bills & Expenses

Due	Bank	Amount Paid	Balance

My monthly trade
S.H.I.F.**T.** goals

_____
_____
_____
_____
_____
_____
_____
_____
_____
_____
_____
_____
_____
_____
_____
_____
_____

My top 3 priorities are...
_____
_____

Trade

Occupation ∴ Education ∴ Parenting ∴ Tasks

Goals:

Priorities:

- [ ]
- [ ]
- [ ]
- [ ]
- [ ]
- [ ]
- [ ]
- [ ]
- [ ]
- [ ]
- [ ]
- [ ]

Deadlines & Dates

{ FEELING OVERWHELMED OR STUCK? **CHUCK IT IN THE F*CK IT BUCKET!** }

Getting my S.H.I.F.T. together today looks like...

Where my S.H.I.F.T. is today...

Gratitude

What brings me peace and happiness?

Reflections on my S.H.I.F.T.

This is how I S.H.I.F.T.

Sprituality _____

_____
_____
_____

Health _____

_____
_____
_____

Interpersonal _____

_____
_____
_____

Finance _____

_____
_____
_____

Trade _____

_____
_____
_____

> *Your biggest fears are your strongest strengths.*
>
> —Dr. Dara

Today my best S.H.I.F.T. looks like:

Gratitude — MY JOY LIST

Today I have my S.H.I.F.T. *together because*...

Today I will keep my S.H.I.F.T. together by...

Gratitude

What am I grateful for today?

I will push the limits of my S.H.I.F.T. by....

S _____

_____

_____

_____

H _____

_____

_____

I _____

_____

_____

F _____

_____

_____

T _____

_____

_____

"
Put your *big girl panties* on!

—Dr. Dara
"

My best S.H.I.F.T. is...

What I need to keep my S.H.I.F.T. together today...

Gratitude : GRATEFUL!

Getting my S.H.I.F.T. together today looks like...

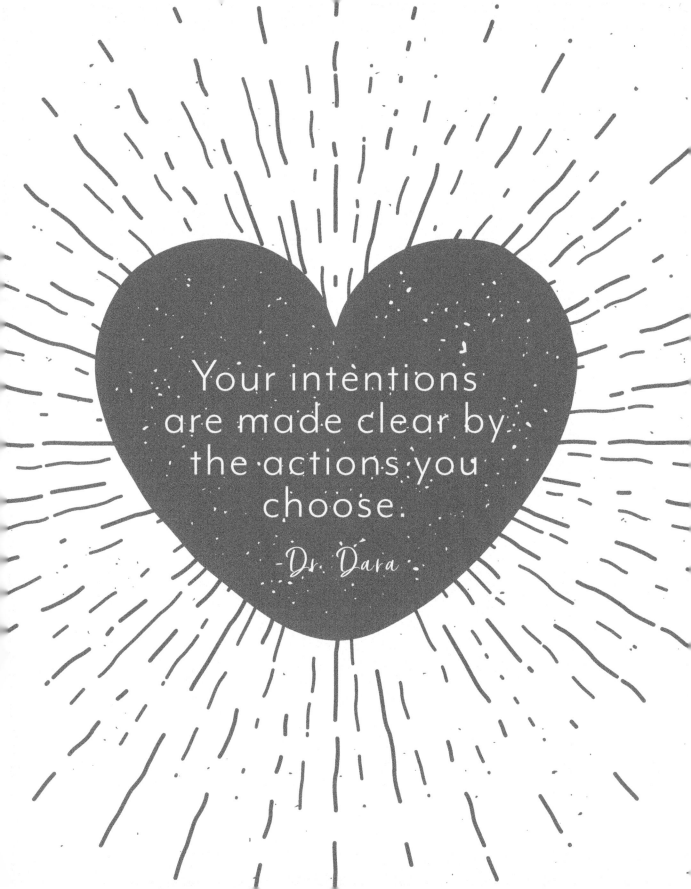

Month _____

Sunday	Monday	Tuesday	Wednesday

20 _____

Thursday	Friday	Saturday

To-DON'TS

Write down any past stuff that's not welcome in your future.

_____
_____
_____
_____
_____
_____
_____

Ta-DAHS

List what is working, what did work, and what you want more of in your future.

_____
_____
_____
_____
_____
_____
_____
_____

Notes

Spirituality

My monthly spiritual **S.**H.I.F.T. goals

_____
_____
_____
_____
_____
_____
_____
_____
_____
_____
_____
_____
_____
_____
_____
_____

I feel most connected spiritually when I...
_____
_____

Spirituality

I am...

Grateful

Health

My monthly health S.**H**.I.F.T. goals

_____
_____
_____
_____
_____
_____
_____
_____
_____
_____
_____
_____
_____
_____
_____
_____
_____
_____

Optimal food choices for me are...
_____
_____

Health

Food · Rest · Exercise

S M T W T F S	nutrition	hours slept	activity	duration
○ ○ ○ ○ ○ ○ ○				
○ ○ ○ ○ ○ ○ ○				
○ ○ ○ ○ ○ ○ ○				
○ ○ ○ ○ ○ ○ ○				
○ ○ ○ ○ ○ ○ ○				
○ ○ ○ ○ ○ ○ ○				
○ ○ ○ ○ ○ ○ ○				
○ ○ ○ ○ ○ ○ ○				
○ ○ ○ ○ ○ ○ ○				
○ ○ ○ ○ ○ ○ ○				
○ ○ ○ ○ ○ ○ ○				
○ ○ ○ ○ ○ ○ ○				
○ ○ ○ ○ ○ ○ ○				
○ ○ ○ ○ ○ ○ ○				
○ ○ ○ ○ ○ ○ ○				
○ ○ ○ ○ ○ ○ ○				

healthy meal ideas: _____

_____

self-care appointments this month: _____

_____

medical appointments this month: _____

_____

Interpersonal

My monthly interpersonal S.H.**I**.F.T. goals

_____
_____
_____
_____
_____
_____
_____
_____
_____
_____
_____
_____
_____
_____
_____
_____
_____
_____

Who helps fill my love cup…
_____
_____

Interpersonal

Goals for this month

- Hobbies:
- Vacation plans:
- Time with:
- I feel best when:
- Activities with friends:
- Self-care:
- Self-enrichment:
- Alone time:
- Activities with family:
- Getting out of my comfort zone:
- Date night ideas:

Finance

My monthly finance S.H.I.**F**.T. goals

_____
_____
_____
_____
_____
_____
_____
_____
_____
_____
_____
_____
_____
_____
_____
_____
_____

My retirement plans...
_____
_____

Finance · Budget · Savings

Income

Date	Service	Amount

Savings

Date	Deposit	Paid Date	Balance

Monthly

Total Income	
Total Budget	
Total Savings	
Total Expenses	

$$ Goals:

Debt

Due	Bank	Amount Paid	Balance

Bills & Expenses

Due	Bank	Amount Paid	Balance

My monthly trade
S.H.I.F.**T.** goals

_____
_____
_____
_____
_____
_____
_____
_____
_____
_____
_____
_____
_____
_____
_____
_____
_____

I am happiest when...
_____
_____

Trade

Occupation • Education • Parenting • Tasks

Goals:

Priorities:

Deadlines & Dates

{ WHEN IT SUCKS, OR YOU ARE NOT SURE
CHUCK IT IN THE F*CK IT BUCKET! }

Getting my S.H.I.F.T. together today looks like...

Where my S.H.I.F.T. is today...

Gratitude

Wow! This happened...

Reflections on my S.H.I.F.T.

This is how I S.H.I.F.T.

Sprituality _____

_____

_____

Health _____

_____

_____

Interpersonal _____

_____

_____

Finance _____

_____

_____

Trade _____

_____

_____

> *Live your truth, your beauty, & your goodness.*
>
> No one else can live it for you.
>
> —Dr. Dara

Today my best S.H.I.F.T. looks like:

Gratitude | I DID THIS...

Today I have my S.H.I.F.T. *together because*...

Take a coloring break

Today I will keep my S.H.I.F.T. together by...

Gratitude

I am grateful to feel, see, know...

I will push the limits of my S.H.I.F.T. by....

S

H

I

F

T

> **Nothing** is going to change if **nothing** changes.
>
> —Dr. Dara

My best S.H.I.F.T. is...

What I need to keep my S.H.I.F.T. together today...

Gratitude — Today I am proud of myself for...

Getting my S.H.I.F.T. together today looks like...

> You can't pour from an empty love cup.
>
> —Dr. Dara

Month _____

Sunday	Monday	Tuesday	Wednesday

20 ⎯⎯⎯

Thursday	Friday	Saturday

To-DON'TS

Write down any past stuff that's not welcome in your future.

_____
_____
_____
_____
_____
_____
_____
_____

Ta-DAHS

List what is working, what did work, and what you want more of in your future.

_____
_____
_____
_____
_____
_____
_____
_____

Notes

Spirituality

My monthly spiritual **S.**H.I.F.T. goals

_____
_____
_____
_____
_____
_____
_____
_____
_____
_____
_____
_____
_____
_____
_____
_____
_____
_____

I feel close to God or my higher power when...
_____
_____

Spirituality

I am...

Inspired

Health

My monthly health S.**H**.I.F.T. goals

_____
_____
_____
_____
_____
_____
_____
_____
_____
_____
_____
_____
_____
_____
_____
_____
_____
_____

To show up as my best self, optimal rest looks like..
_____
_____

Health

Food · Rest · Exercise

S	M	T	W	T	F	S	nutrition	hours slept	activity	duration
○	○	○	○	○	○	○				
○	○	○	○	○	○	○				
○	○	○	○	○	○	○				
○	○	○	○	○	○	○				
○	○	○	○	○	○	○				
○	○	○	○	○	○	○				
○	○	○	○	○	○	○				
○	○	○	○	○	○	○				
○	○	○	○	○	○	○				
○	○	○	○	○	○	○				
○	○	○	○	○	○	○				
○	○	○	○	○	○	○				
○	○	○	○	○	○	○				
○	○	○	○	○	○	○				
○	○	○	○	○	○	○				

healthy meal ideas: _____
_____

self-care appointments this month: _____
_____

medical appointments this month: _____
_____

Interpersonal

My monthly interpersonal S.H.**I**.F.T. goals

_____
_____
_____
_____
_____
_____
_____
_____
_____
_____
_____
_____
_____
_____
_____

Fun to me is...
_____
_____

Finance

My monthly finance S.H.I.**F**.T. goals

_____
_____
_____
_____
_____
_____
_____
_____
_____
_____
_____
_____
_____
_____
_____
_____
_____

A spending/money habit that I can improve is...
_____
_____

Finance

Finance :: Budget :: Savings

Income

Date	Service	Amount

Savings

Date	Deposit	Paid Date	Balance

Monthly

Total Income	
Total Budget	
Total Savings	
Total Expenses	

$$ Goals:

Debt

Due	Bank	Amount Paid	Balance

Bills & Expenses

Due	Bank	Amount Paid	Balance

Trade

My monthly trade S.H.I.F.**T.** goals

_____
_____
_____
_____
_____
_____
_____
_____
_____
_____
_____
_____
_____
_____
_____
_____
_____
_____
_____
_____

Success looks like...
_____
_____

Trade

Occupation · Education · Parenting · Tasks

Goals:

Priorities:

Deadlines & Dates

{ BECAUSE WHEN YOU THINK YOU HAVE TO DO SOMETHING—DO NOTHING }
CHUCK IT IN THE F*CK IT BUCKET!

Getting my S.H.I.F.T. together today looks like…

Where my S.H.I.F.T. *is today*...

Gratitude

This is how I am blessed...

Reflections on my S.H.I.F.T.

This is how I S.H.I.F.T.

Sprituality

Health

Interpersonal

Finance

Trade

> *Vulnerability is connection.*
>
> —Dr. Dara

Today my best S.H.I.F.T. looks like:

Gratitude : TODAY I GET TO...

Today I have my S.H.I.F.T. *together because*...

Today I will keep my S.H.I.F.T. together by...

Gratitude

I am grateful for my body because...

I will push the limits of my S.H.I.F.T. by....

S

H

I

F

T

"

All I have
to do today is
show up.

-Dr. Dara

"

My best S.H.I.F.T. is...

What I need to keep my S.H.I.F.T. together today…

Gratitude — THANK YOU FOR...

Getting my S.H.I.F.T. together today looks like...

___

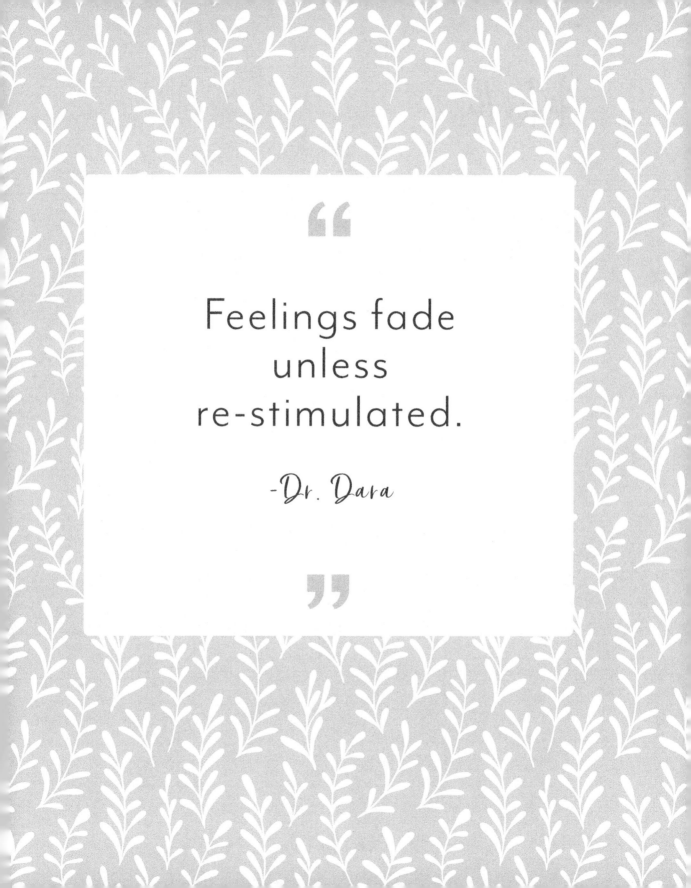

Sunday	Monday	Tuesday	Wednesday

20 _____

Thursday	Friday	Saturday

To-DON'TS

Write down any past stuff that's not welcome in your future.

_____
_____
_____
_____
_____
_____
_____
_____

Ta-DAHS

List what is working, what did work, and what you want more of in your future.

_____
_____
_____
_____
_____
_____
_____
_____

Notes

Spirituality

My monthly spiritual **S.**H.I.F.T. goals

_____
_____
_____
_____
_____
_____
_____
_____
_____
_____
_____
_____
_____
_____
_____
_____
_____

I feel most spiritually connected when I spend time with...

_____
_____

Spirituality

I am...

Loving

S.H.I.F.T. for an Unapologetically Kick-Ass Life

Health

My monthly health
S.**H**.I.F.T. goals

_____
_____
_____
_____
_____
_____
_____
_____
_____
_____
_____
_____
_____
_____
_____
_____
_____
_____
_____
_____

My food, exercise and rest goals are...
_____
_____

Health

Food · Rest · Exercise

S M T W T F S	nutrition	hours slept	activity	duration
○ ○ ○ ○ ○ ○ ○				
○ ○ ○ ○ ○ ○ ○				
○ ○ ○ ○ ○ ○ ○				
○ ○ ○ ○ ○ ○ ○				
○ ○ ○ ○ ○ ○ ○				
○ ○ ○ ○ ○ ○ ○				
○ ○ ○ ○ ○ ○ ○				
○ ○ ○ ○ ○ ○ ○				
○ ○ ○ ○ ○ ○ ○				
○ ○ ○ ○ ○ ○ ○				
○ ○ ○ ○ ○ ○ ○				
○ ○ ○ ○ ○ ○ ○				
○ ○ ○ ○ ○ ○ ○				
○ ○ ○ ○ ○ ○ ○				
○ ○ ○ ○ ○ ○ ○				
○ ○ ○ ○ ○ ○ ○				

healthy meal ideas: _____
_____

self-care appointments this month: _____
_____

medical appointments this month: _____
_____

Interpersonal

My monthly interpersonal S.H.**I**.F.T. goals

_____
_____
_____
_____
_____
_____
_____
_____
_____
_____
_____
_____
_____
_____
_____
_____

I am my best self when I am around...

_____
_____

Interpersonal

Goals for this month

Finance

My monthly finance S.H.I.**F**.T. goals

I can increase my weekly savings by...

Finance

Finance · Budget · Savings

Income

Date	Service	Amount

Debt

Due	Bank	Amount Paid	Balance

Savings

Date	Deposit	Paid Date	Balance

Monthly

Total Income	
Total Budget	
Total Savings	
Total Expenses	

Bills & Expenses

Due	Bank	Amount Paid	Balance

$$ Goals:

My monthly trade
S.H.I.F.**T.** goals

_____
_____
_____
_____
_____
_____
_____
_____
_____
_____
_____
_____
_____
_____
_____
_____
_____
_____
_____

I am most proud of...
_____
_____

Trade

Occupation ∴ Education ∴ Parenting ∴ Tasks

Goals:

Priorities:

Deadlines & Dates

{ IF YOU SQUINT YOUR EYES AND COCK YOUR HEAD... YOU DON'T KNOW **PUT IT IN THE F*CK IT BUCKET!** }

Getting my S.H.I.F.T. together today looks like...

Where my S.H.I.F.T. is today...

Gratitude

Today I am grateful to feel...

Reflections on my S.H.I.F.T.

This is how I S.H.I.F.T.

Sprituality _____

Health _____

Interpersonal _____

Finance _____

Trade _____

> "Taking time
> to connect
> with nature
> nurtures the soul.
>
> —Dr. Dara"

Today my best S.H.I.F.T. looks like:

Gratitude : THANK YOU FOR...

Today I have my S.H.I.F.T. *together because*...

Today I will keep my S.H.I.F.T. together by...

Gratitude

Yay me because I....

_____
_____
_____
_____
_____

_____
_____
_____
_____
_____
_____
_____
_____
_____
_____
_____
_____
_____
_____
_____

I will push the limits of my S.H.I.F.T. by....

S ___

H ___

I ___

F ___

T ___

> Trying to control your thoughts is like trying to stop a moving train-you can't. Let it ride through!
>
> —Dr. Dara

My best S.H.I.F.T. is...

What I need to keep my S.H.I.F.T. together today...

Gratitude | TODAY I GOT TO...

Getting my S.H.I.F.T. together today looks like...

Month _____

Sunday	Monday	Tuesday	Wednesday

20 _____

Thursday	Friday	Saturday

To-DON'TS

Write down any past stuff that's not welcome in your future.

_____
_____
_____
_____
_____
_____
_____
_____

Ta-DAHS

List what is working, what did work, and what you want more of in your future.

_____
_____
_____
_____
_____
_____
_____
_____

Notes

Spirituality

My monthly spiritual
S.H.I.F.T. goals

_____
_____
_____
_____
_____
_____
_____
_____
_____
_____
_____
_____
_____
_____
_____
_____
_____
_____
_____

Spirituality to me is...
_____
_____

Spirituality

I am...

Beautiful

Health

My monthly health S.**H**.I.F.T. goals

_____
_____
_____
_____
_____
_____
_____
_____
_____
_____
_____
_____
_____
_____
_____
_____
_____
_____

My strongest body needs...
_____
_____

Health

Food · Rest · Exercise

S	M	T	W	T	F	S	nutrition	hours slept	activity	duration
○	○	○	○	○	○	○				
○	○	○	○	○	○	○				
○	○	○	○	○	○	○				
○	○	○	○	○	○	○				
○	○	○	○	○	○	○				
○	○	○	○	○	○	○				
○	○	○	○	○	○	○				
○	○	○	○	○	○	○				
○	○	○	○	○	○	○				
○	○	○	○	○	○	○				
○	○	○	○	○	○	○				
○	○	○	○	○	○	○				
○	○	○	○	○	○	○				
○	○	○	○	○	○	○				
○	○	○	○	○	○	○				

healthy meal ideas: _____
_____

self-care appointments this month: _____
_____

medical appointments this month: _____
_____

Interpersonal

My monthly interpersonal S.H.**I**.F.T. goals

_____
_____
_____
_____
_____
_____
_____
_____
_____
_____
_____
_____
_____
_____
_____

Who fuels my spirit?
_____
_____

Interpersonal

Goals for this month

- Hobbies:
- Vacation plans:
- Time with:
- I feel best when:
- Activities with friends:
- Self-care:
- Alone time:
- Self-enrichment:
- Date night ideas:
- Activities with family:
- Getting out of my comfort zone:

Finance

My monthly finance S.H.I.**F**.T. goals

My relationship with money feels like...

Finance

Finance · Budget · Savings

Income

Date	Service	Amount

Savings

Date	Deposit	Paid Date	Balance

Monthly

Total Income	
Total Budget	
Total Savings	
Total Expenses	

$$ Goals:

Debt

Due	Bank	Amount Paid	Balance

Bills & Expenses

Due	Bank	Amount Paid	Balance

Trade

My monthly trade S.H.I.F.**T.** goals

_____
_____
_____
_____
_____
_____
_____
_____
_____
_____
_____
_____
_____
_____
_____
_____
_____
_____

My strengths are...
_____
_____

Trade

Occupation ∴ Education ∴ Parenting ∴ Tasks

Goals:

Priorities:

Deadlines & Dates

{ NOT SURE WHAT TO DO NEXT, PAUSE IT
CHUCK IT IN THE F*CK IT BUCKET
AND LET THE UNCERTAINTY DRIP OFF }

Getting my S.H.I.F.T. together today looks like...

Where my S.H.I.F.T. *is today*...

Gratitude

Grateful to keep my S.H.I.F.T. together...

Reflections on my S.H.I.F.T.

This is how I S.H.I.F.T.

Sprituality _____

Health _____

Interpersonal _____

Finance _____

Trade _____

"

Laughter
is oxygen
for the soul.

—Dr. Dara

"

Today my best S.H.I.F.T. looks like:

Gratitude : I AM ME BECAUSE...

Today I have my S.H.I.F.T. *together because*...

Today I will keep my S.H.I.F.T. together by...

Gratitude

I am my best self because...

I will push the limits of my S.H.I.F.T. by....

S ———

H ———

I ———

F ———

T ———

"

How you take care
of **yourself** is how you
show up for **others**.

–Dr. Dara

"

My best S.H.I.F.T. is...

What I need to keep my S.H.I.F.T. together today...

Gratitude

Today I showed up in a big way by...

Getting my S.H.I.F.T. together today looks like...

> Stop taking yourself so seriously, because no one else is!
>
> —Dr. Dara

Month _____

Sunday	Monday	Tuesday	Wednesday

20 ———

Thursday	Friday	Saturday

To-DON'TS

Write down any past stuff that's not welcome in your future.

_____
_____
_____
_____
_____
_____
_____
_____

Ta-DAHS

List what is working, what did work, and what you want more of in your future.

_____
_____
_____
_____
_____
_____
_____
_____

Notes

Spirituality

My monthly spiritual **S.**H.I.F.T. goals

_____
_____
_____
_____
_____
_____
_____
_____
_____
_____
_____
_____
_____
_____
_____
_____

I find personal growth by...
_____
_____

Spirituality

I am...

Kind

Health

My monthly health S.**H**.I.F.T. goals

_____
_____
_____
_____
_____
_____
_____
_____
_____
_____
_____
_____
_____
_____
_____
_____
_____
_____
_____

An optimal relationship for me with food, exercise and rest looks like...
_____
_____

Health

Food · Rest · Exercise

S M T W T F S	nutrition	hours slept	activity	duration
○ ○ ○ ○ ○ ○ ○				
○ ○ ○ ○ ○ ○ ○				
○ ○ ○ ○ ○ ○ ○				
○ ○ ○ ○ ○ ○ ○				
○ ○ ○ ○ ○ ○ ○				
○ ○ ○ ○ ○ ○ ○				
○ ○ ○ ○ ○ ○ ○				
○ ○ ○ ○ ○ ○ ○				
○ ○ ○ ○ ○ ○ ○				
○ ○ ○ ○ ○ ○ ○				
○ ○ ○ ○ ○ ○ ○				
○ ○ ○ ○ ○ ○ ○				
○ ○ ○ ○ ○ ○ ○				
○ ○ ○ ○ ○ ○ ○				
○ ○ ○ ○ ○ ○ ○				
○ ○ ○ ○ ○ ○ ○				

healthy meal ideas: _____
_____

self-care appointments this month: _____
_____

medical appointments this month: _____
_____

Interpersonal

My monthly interpersonal S.H.**I**.F.T. goals

_____
_____
_____
_____
_____
_____
_____
_____
_____
_____
_____
_____
_____
_____
_____

Optimal time with my family looks like...
_____
_____

Interpersonal

Goals for this month

Finance

My monthly finance S.H.I.**F**.T. goals

_____
_____
_____
_____
_____
_____
_____
_____
_____
_____
_____
_____
_____
_____
_____
_____
_____
_____
_____

Ideas to consolidate and eliminate debt:
_____
_____

Finance

Finance · Budget · Savings

Income

Date	Service	Amount

Savings

Date	Deposit	Paid Date	Balance

Monthly

Total Income	
Total Budget	
Total Savings	
Total Expenses	

$$ Goals:

Debt

Due	Bank	Amount Paid	Balance

Bills & Expenses

Due	Bank	Amount Paid	Balance

My monthly trade
S.H.I.F.**T.** goals

I can optimize...

Trade

Occupation · Education · Parenting · Tasks

Goals:

Priorities:

Deadlines & Dates

{ SHOULDING ALL OVER YOURSELF? TIRED OF DOING WHAT EVERYONE ELSE THINKS YOU SHOULD? **CHUCK IT IN THE F*CK IT BUCKET** AND LET IT SIMMER DOWN. }

Getting my **S.H.I.F.T.** together today looks like...

Where my S.H.I.F.T. is *today*...

Gratitude

I am grateful my body can...

Reflections on my S.H.I.F.T.

This is how I S.H.I.F.T.

Sprituality ___

Health ___

Interpersonal ___

Finance ___

Trade ___

> *Progress* not *perfection.*
> —Dr. Dara

Today my best S.H.I.F.T. looks like:

Gratitude

My S.H.I.F.T. is clear because I...

Today I have my S.H.I.F.T. *together because*...

Today I will keep my S.H.I.F.T. together by...

Gratitude

I am my best self when...

I will push the limits of my S.H.I.F.T. by....

S _____

_____

_____

H _____

_____

_____

I _____

_____

_____

F _____

_____

_____

T _____

_____

_____

> The world I see outside myself is a reflection of the world I have shaped within.
> The world I experience is an extension of my mind, heart, and spirit.
>
> —Dr. Dara

My best S.H.I.F.T. is...

What I need to keep my S.H.I.F.T. together today...

Gratitude

I am my best self because...

Getting my S.H.I.F.T. together today looks like...

"
The moment an
idea becomes an
option—S.H.I.F.T.

-Dr. Dara

"

Month _____

Sunday	Monday	Tuesday	Wednesday

20 ———

Thursday	Friday	Saturday

To-DON'TS

Write down any past stuff that's not welcome in your future.

Ta-DAHS

List what is working, what did work, and what you want more of in your future.

Notes

Spirituality

My monthly spiritual **S.**H.I.F.T. goals

_____
_____
_____
_____
_____
_____
_____
_____
_____
_____
_____
_____
_____
_____
_____
_____
_____

Meditation for me looks like...
_____
_____

Spirituality

I am...

Prosperous

Health

My monthly health S.**H**.I.F.T. goals

_____
_____
_____
_____
_____
_____
_____
_____
_____
_____
_____
_____
_____
_____
_____
_____
_____
_____
_____

I am at maximum energy when I....
_____
_____

Health

Food · Rest · Exercise

S M T W T F S	nutrition	hours slept	activity	duration
○ ○ ○ ○ ○ ○ ○				
○ ○ ○ ○ ○ ○ ○				
○ ○ ○ ○ ○ ○ ○				
○ ○ ○ ○ ○ ○ ○				
○ ○ ○ ○ ○ ○ ○				
○ ○ ○ ○ ○ ○ ○				
○ ○ ○ ○ ○ ○ ○				
○ ○ ○ ○ ○ ○ ○				
○ ○ ○ ○ ○ ○ ○				
○ ○ ○ ○ ○ ○ ○				
○ ○ ○ ○ ○ ○ ○				
○ ○ ○ ○ ○ ○ ○				
○ ○ ○ ○ ○ ○ ○				
○ ○ ○ ○ ○ ○ ○				
○ ○ ○ ○ ○ ○ ○				
○ ○ ○ ○ ○ ○ ○				

healthy meal ideas: _____
_____

self-care appointments this month: _____
_____

medical appointments this month: _____
_____

Interpersonal

My monthly interpersonal S.H.**I**.F.T. goals

_____
_____
_____
_____
_____
_____
_____
_____
_____
_____
_____
_____
_____
_____
_____
_____

My ideal party and social event calendar looks like...
_____
_____

Interpersonal

Goals for this month

Finance

My monthly finance S.H.I.**F**.T. goals

My 1 year savings plan will provide me with...

Finance

Finance · Budget · Savings

Income

Date	Service	Amount

Savings

Date	Deposit	Paid Date	Balance

Monthly

Total Income	
Total Budget	
Total Savings	
Total Expenses	

$$ Goals:

Debt

Due	Bank	Amount Paid	Balance

Bills & Expenses

Due	Bank	Amount Paid	Balance

Trade

My monthly trade S.H.I.F.**T.** goals

_____
_____
_____
_____
_____
_____
_____
_____
_____
_____
_____
_____
_____
_____
_____
_____
_____

I can optimize my time management by
_____
_____

Trade

Occupation ∴ Education ∴ Parenting ∴ Tasks

Goals:

Priorities:

Deadlines & Dates

{ FEEL DAMNED IF YOU DO AND DAMNED IF YOU DON'T?
SLAM THE DAMN IN THE BUCKET FOR 24 HOURS! }

Getting my S.H.I.F.T. together today looks like...

Where my S.H.I.F.T. *is today*...

Gratitude

What brings me peace and happiness?

Reflections on my S.H.I.F.T.

This is how I S.H.I.F.T.

Sprituality

Health

Interpersonal

Finance

Trade

Today my best S.H.I.F.T. looks like:

Gratitude : MY JOY LIST

Today I have my S.H.I.F.T. *together because*...

Take a coloring break

Today I will keep my S.H.I.F.T. together by...

Gratitude

What am I grateful for today?

I will push the limits of my S.H.I.F.T. by....

S

H

I

F

T

If you have to squint your eyes, cock your head, squeeze your jaw, or mutter, "Mmmmm" to make a decision, the answer is **NO!**

—Dr. Dara

My best S.H.I.F.T. is...

What I need to keep my S.H.I.F.T. together today...

Gratitude

5 things I am grateful for today...

Getting my S.H.I.F.T. together today looks like…

Grace

humbles you and allows a profound path to true self reflection and being.

—Dr. Dara

Month _____

Sunday	Monday	Tuesday	Wednesday

20 _____

Thursday	Friday	Saturday

To-DON'TS

Write down any past stuff that's not welcome in your future.

_____
_____
_____
_____
_____
_____
_____

Ta-DAHS

List what is working, what did work, and what you want more of in your future.

_____
_____
_____
_____
_____
_____
_____

Notes

Spirituality

My monthly spiritual **S.**H.I.F.T. goals

_____
_____
_____
_____
_____
_____
_____
_____
_____
_____
_____
_____
_____
_____
_____
_____
_____

I am most peaceful when I am spiritually...
_____
_____

Spirituality

I am...

Strong

S.H.I.F.T. for an Unapologetically Kick-Ass Life

Health

My monthly health S.**H**.I.F.T. goals

_____
_____
_____
_____
_____
_____
_____
_____
_____
_____
_____
_____
_____
_____
_____
_____
_____
_____
_____
_____

Medical appointments for me to make are....
_____
_____

Health

Food · Rest · Exercise

S M T W T F S	nutrition	hours slept	activity	duration
○ ○ ○ ○ ○ ○ ○				
○ ○ ○ ○ ○ ○ ○				
○ ○ ○ ○ ○ ○ ○				
○ ○ ○ ○ ○ ○ ○				
○ ○ ○ ○ ○ ○ ○				
○ ○ ○ ○ ○ ○ ○				
○ ○ ○ ○ ○ ○ ○				
○ ○ ○ ○ ○ ○ ○				
○ ○ ○ ○ ○ ○ ○				
○ ○ ○ ○ ○ ○ ○				
○ ○ ○ ○ ○ ○ ○				
○ ○ ○ ○ ○ ○ ○				
○ ○ ○ ○ ○ ○ ○				
○ ○ ○ ○ ○ ○ ○				
○ ○ ○ ○ ○ ○ ○				
○ ○ ○ ○ ○ ○ ○				

healthy meal ideas: _____
_____

self-care appointments this month: _____
_____

medical appointments this month: _____
_____

Interpersonal

My monthly interpersonal S.H.**I**.F.T. goals

_____
_____
_____
_____
_____
_____
_____
_____
_____
_____
_____
_____
_____
_____
_____

How much more income will make me happy...
_____
_____

Finance

My monthly finance S.H.I.**F**.T. goals

_____
_____
_____
_____
_____
_____
_____
_____
_____
_____
_____
_____
_____
_____
_____
_____
_____
_____
_____

My ideal routine...
_____
_____

Finance

Finance · Budget · Savings

Income

Date	Service	Amount

Savings

Date	Deposit	Paid Date	Balance

Monthly

Total Income	
Total Budget	
Total Savings	
Total Expenses	

$$ Goals:

Debt

Due	Bank	Amount Paid	Balance

Bills & Expenses

Due	Bank	Amount Paid	Balance

My monthly trade
S.H.I.F.**T.** goals

_____
_____
_____
_____
_____
_____
_____
_____
_____
_____
_____
_____
_____
_____
_____
_____
_____
_____
_____
_____
_____
_____
_____

I am happiest when...
_____
_____

Trade

Occupation ∴ Education ∴ Parenting ∴ Tasks

Goals:

Priorities:

Deadlines & Dates

{ DOING NOTHING IS DOING EVERYTHING!
CHUCK IT IN THE F*CK IT BUCKET!
FOR 24 HOURS AND THEN REASSESS
THE PRIORITY! }

Getting my S.H.I.F.T. together today looks like...

Where my S.H.I.F.T. is *today*...

Gratitude

Wow! This happened...

Reflections on my S.H.I.F.T.

This is how I S.H.I.F.T.

Sprituality

Health

Interpersonal

Finance

Trade

" *You are who you surround yourself with. Smother yourself with wonderfuls.*

—Dr. Dara
"

Today my best S.H.I.F.T. looks like:

Gratitude | I DID THIS...

Today I have my S.H.I.F.T. *together because*...

Take a coloring break

Today I will keep my S.H.I.F.T. together by...

Gratitude

I am grateful to feel, see, know...

I will push the limits of my S.H.I.F.T. by....

S ___

H ___

I ___

F ___

T ___

> The problem is not **what** you are thinking, it is **how** you are thinking about **what** you are thinking.
>
> —Dr. Dara

My best S.H.I.F.T. is...

What I need to keep my S.H.I.F.T. together today...

Gratitude — Today I am proud of...

Getting my S.H.I.F.T. together today looks like...

> Some things are bigger than you. Show up with inquisition and interest.
>
> —Dr. Dara

Month _____

Sunday	Monday	Tuesday	Wednesday

20 _____

Thursday	Friday	Saturday

To-DON'TS

Write down any past stuff that's not welcome in your future.

_____
_____
_____
_____
_____
_____

Ta-DAHS

List what is working, what did work, and what you want more of in your future.

_____
_____
_____
_____
_____
_____
_____

Notes

Spirituality

My monthly spiritual **S.**H.I.F.T. goals

_____
_____
_____
_____
_____
_____
_____
_____
_____
_____
_____
_____
_____
_____
_____
_____
_____
_____
_____

Spending time alone to spiritually connect looks like...
_____
_____

Spirituality

I am...

Brave

My monthly health
S.**H**.I.F.T. goals

_____
_____
_____
_____
_____
_____
_____
_____
_____
_____
_____
_____
_____
_____
_____
_____
_____
_____
_____

I define my self-care as...
_____
_____

Health

Food · Rest · Exercise

S M T W T F S	nutrition	hours slept	activity	duration
○ ○ ○ ○ ○ ○ ○				
○ ○ ○ ○ ○ ○ ○				
○ ○ ○ ○ ○ ○ ○				
○ ○ ○ ○ ○ ○ ○				
○ ○ ○ ○ ○ ○ ○				
○ ○ ○ ○ ○ ○ ○				
○ ○ ○ ○ ○ ○ ○				
○ ○ ○ ○ ○ ○ ○				
○ ○ ○ ○ ○ ○ ○				
○ ○ ○ ○ ○ ○ ○				
○ ○ ○ ○ ○ ○ ○				
○ ○ ○ ○ ○ ○ ○				
○ ○ ○ ○ ○ ○ ○				
○ ○ ○ ○ ○ ○ ○				
○ ○ ○ ○ ○ ○ ○				

healthy meal ideas: _____
_____

self-care appointments this month: _____
_____

medical appointments this month: _____
_____

Interpersonal

My monthly interpersonal S.H.**I**.F.T. goals

_____
_____
_____
_____
_____
_____
_____
_____
_____
_____
_____
_____
_____
_____
_____
_____
_____

Ideal alone time looks like...
_____
_____

Interpersonal

Goals for this month

- Hobbies:
- Vacation plans:
- Time with:
- I feel best when:
- Activities with friends:
- Self-care:
- Self-enrichment:
- Alone time:
- Activities with family:
- Date night ideas:
- Getting out of my comfort zone:

Finance

My monthly finance S.H.I.**F**.T. goals

_____
_____
_____
_____
_____
_____
_____
_____
_____
_____
_____
_____
_____
_____
_____
_____
_____

When I look at my bank account I feel...
_____
_____

Finance

Finance · Budget · Savings

Income

Date	Service	Amount

Savings

Date	Deposit	Paid Date	Balance

Monthly

Total Income	
Total Budget	
Total Savings	
Total Expenses	

$$ Goals:

Debt

Due	Bank	Amount Paid	Balance

Bills & Expenses

Due	Bank	Amount Paid	Balance

Trade

My monthly trade S.H.I.F.**T.** goals

My motivation to improve my goals...

Trade

Occupation · Education · Parenting · Tasks

Goals:

Priorities:

Deadlines & Dates

{ NOTHING IS THAT URGENT! EVERYONE ELSE'S EMERGENCIES AND DRAMAS ARE NOT YOURS! }
HELLO F*CK IT BUCKET!

Getting my S.H.I.F.T. together today looks like...

Where my S.H.I.F.T. is today...

Gratitude

This is how I am blessed...

Reflections on my S.H.I.F.T.

This is how I S.H.I.F.T.

Sprituality

Health

Interpersonal

Finance

Trade

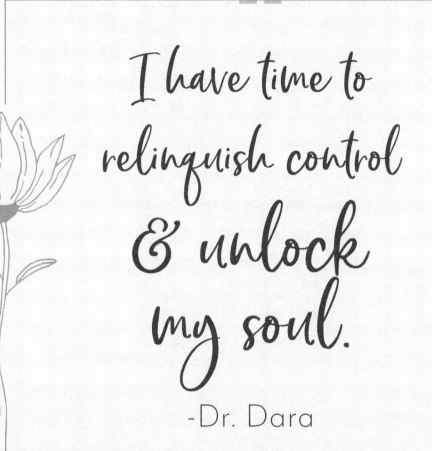

> "I have time to relinquish control & unlock my soul."
>
> —Dr. Dara

Today my best S.H.I.F.T. looks like:

Gratitude | TODAY I GET TO...

Today I have my S.H.I.F.T. *together because*...

Take a coloring break

Today I will keep my S.H.I.F.T. together by...

Gratitude

I am grateful for my body...

I will push the limits of my S.H.I.F.T. by....

S

H

I

F

T

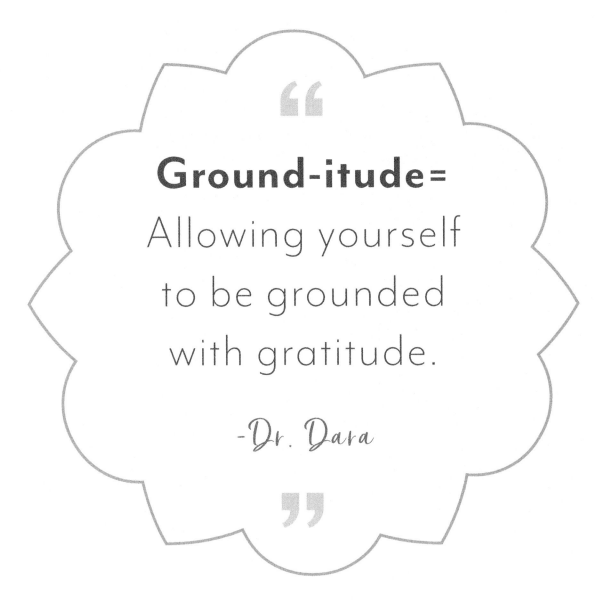

"**Ground-itude=** Allowing yourself to be grounded with gratitude.

-Dr. Dara"

My best S.H.I.F.T. is...

What I need to keep my S.H.I.F.T. together today...

Gratitude : THANK YOU FOR…

Getting my S.H.I.F.T. together today looks like...

> "I don't need permission to play. I choose joy. *I choose fun.*
>
> —Dr. Dara"

Month

Sunday	Monday	Tuesday	Wednesday

20 ———

Thursday	Friday	Saturday

To-DON'TS

Write down any past stuff that's not welcome in your future.

_____
_____
_____
_____
_____
_____
_____

Ta-DAHS

List what is working, what did work, and what you want more of in your future.

_____
_____
_____
_____
_____
_____
_____

Notes

Spirituality

My monthly spiritual
S.H.I.F.T. goals

_____
_____
_____
_____
_____
_____
_____
_____
_____
_____
_____
_____
_____
_____
_____
_____
_____

To feel connected spiritually, I (write, do yoga, meditate, pray)...
_____
_____

Spirituality

I am...

Enough

S.H.I.F.T. for an Unapologetically Kick-Ass Life

Health

My monthly health S.**H**.I.F.T. goals

_____
_____
_____
_____
_____
_____
_____
_____
_____
_____
_____
_____
_____
_____
_____
_____
_____
_____
_____
_____

My health is optimized when I...
_____
_____

Health

Food ∴ Rest ∴ Exercise

S M T W T F S	nutrition	hours slept	activity	duration
○ ○ ○ ○ ○ ○ ○				
○ ○ ○ ○ ○ ○ ○				
○ ○ ○ ○ ○ ○ ○				
○ ○ ○ ○ ○ ○ ○				
○ ○ ○ ○ ○ ○ ○				
○ ○ ○ ○ ○ ○ ○				
○ ○ ○ ○ ○ ○ ○				
○ ○ ○ ○ ○ ○ ○				
○ ○ ○ ○ ○ ○ ○				
○ ○ ○ ○ ○ ○ ○				
○ ○ ○ ○ ○ ○ ○				
○ ○ ○ ○ ○ ○ ○				
○ ○ ○ ○ ○ ○ ○				
○ ○ ○ ○ ○ ○ ○				
○ ○ ○ ○ ○ ○ ○				

healthy meal ideas: _____
_____

self-care appointments this month: _____
_____

medical appointments this month: _____
_____

Interpersonal

My monthly interpersonal S.H.**I**.F.T. goals

_____
_____
_____
_____
_____
_____
_____
_____
_____
_____
_____
_____
_____
_____

My perfect Date night with a significant other or friend is...
_____
_____

Finance

My monthly finance S.H.I.**F**.T. goals

_____
_____
_____
_____
_____
_____
_____
_____
_____
_____
_____
_____
_____
_____
_____
_____

In 10 years, I will be able to afford...
_____
_____

Finance

Finance · Budget · Savings

Income

Date	Service	Amount

Savings

Date	Deposit	Paid Date	Balance

Monthly

Total Income	
Total Budget	
Total Savings	
Total Expenses	

$$ Goals:

Debt

Due	Bank	Amount Paid	Balance

Bills & Expenses

Due	Bank	Amount Paid	Balance

My monthly trade
S.H.I.F.**T.** goals

_____
_____
_____
_____
_____
_____
_____
_____
_____
_____
_____
_____
_____
_____
_____
_____
_____
_____
_____
_____

My ideal role...
_____
_____

Trade

Occupation ∴ Education ∴ Parenting ∴ Tasks

Goals:

Priorities:

Deadlines & Dates

{ IF YOU SQUINT YOUR EYES AND COCK YOUR HEAD… YOU DON'T KNOW **PUT IT IN THE F*CK IT BUCKET!** }

Getting my S.H.I.F.T. together today looks like...

Where my S.H.I.F.T. *is* today...

Gratitude

Today I am grateful to feel...

Reflections on my S.H.I.F.T.

This is how I S.H.I.F.T.

Sprituality

Health

Interpersonal

Finance

Trade

> *Because, today, I am more than perfect. I am perfectly imperfectly me.*
>
> —Dr. Dara

Today my best S.H.I.F.T. looks like:

Gratitude — THANK YOU FOR...

Today I have my S.H.I.F.T. *together because...*

Take a coloring break

Today I will keep my S.H.I.F.T. together by...

Gratitude

Yay me because I....

I will push the limits of my S.H.I.F.T. by....

S

H

I

F

T

"
The little engine
didn't think she could.
She KNEW she
could and
CRUSHED IT!

-Dr. Dara

"

My best S.H.I.F.T. is...

What I need to keep my S.H.I.F.T. together today...

Gratitude | TODAY I GOT TO...

Getting my S.H.I.F.T. together today looks like…

> If you want to know what the future holds, take a solid look at how you are showing up today.
>
> —Dr. Dara

Month _____

Sunday	Monday	Tuesday	Wednesday

20 ———

Thursday	Friday	Saturday

To-DON'TS

Write down any past stuff that's not welcome in your future.

_____
_____
_____
_____
_____
_____
_____
_____

Ta-DAHS

List what is working, what did work, and what you want more of in your future.

_____
_____
_____
_____
_____
_____
_____
_____

Notes

Spirituality

My monthly spiritual **S.**H.I.F.T. goals

_____
_____
_____
_____
_____
_____
_____
_____
_____
_____
_____
_____
_____
_____
_____
_____
_____

I feel the most gratitude and love when...
_____
_____

Spirituality

I am...

Abundant

Health

My monthly health S.**H**.I.F.T. goals

_____
_____
_____
_____
_____
_____
_____
_____
_____
_____
_____
_____
_____
_____
_____
_____
_____

I am my best self when I eat... move... sleep...
_____
_____

Health

Food ∴ Rest ∴ Exercise

S M T W T F S	nutrition	hours slept	activity	duration
○ ○ ○ ○ ○ ○ ○				
○ ○ ○ ○ ○ ○ ○				
○ ○ ○ ○ ○ ○ ○				
○ ○ ○ ○ ○ ○ ○				
○ ○ ○ ○ ○ ○ ○				
○ ○ ○ ○ ○ ○ ○				
○ ○ ○ ○ ○ ○ ○				
○ ○ ○ ○ ○ ○ ○				
○ ○ ○ ○ ○ ○ ○				
○ ○ ○ ○ ○ ○ ○				
○ ○ ○ ○ ○ ○ ○				
○ ○ ○ ○ ○ ○ ○				
○ ○ ○ ○ ○ ○ ○				
○ ○ ○ ○ ○ ○ ○				
○ ○ ○ ○ ○ ○ ○				

healthy meal ideas: _____
_____

self-care appointments this month: _____
_____

medical appointments this month: _____
_____

Interpersonal

My monthly interpersonal S.H.**I**.F.T. goals

_____
_____
_____
_____
_____
_____
_____
_____
_____
_____
_____
_____
_____
_____
_____
_____
_____

I am my happiest when I...
_____
_____

Finance

My monthly finance S.H.I.**F**.T. goals

I feel richest in my life when...

Finance

Finance · Budget · Savings

Income

Date	Service	Amount

Savings

Date	Deposit	Paid Date	Balance

Monthly

Total Income	
Total Budget	
Total Savings	
Total Expenses	

$$ Goals:

Debt

Due	Bank	Amount Paid	Balance

Bills & Expenses

Due	Bank	Amount Paid	Balance

Trade

My monthly trade S.H.I.F.**T.** goals

_____
_____
_____
_____
_____
_____
_____
_____
_____
_____
_____
_____
_____
_____
_____
_____
_____
_____
_____
_____

Distractions that get in my way...

_____
_____

Trade

Occupation ∴ Education ∴ Parenting ∴ Tasks

Goals:

Priorities:

Deadlines & Dates

{ NOT SURE WHAT TO DO NEXT, PAUSE IT **CHUCK IT IN THE F*CK IT BUCKET** AND LET THE UNCERTAINTY DRIP OFF }

Getting my S.H.I.F.T. together today looks like...

Where my S.H.I.F.T. *is today*...

Gratitude

Grateful to keep my S.H.I.F.T. together...

Reflections on my S.H.I.F.T.

This is how I S.H.I.F.T.

Sprituality

_____
_____
_____
_____

Health

_____
_____
_____
_____

Interpersonal

_____
_____
_____
_____

Finance

_____
_____
_____
_____

Trade

_____
_____
_____
_____

> "My *choices* today are my *intentions* for tomorrow.
>
> —Dr. Dara"

Today my best S.H.I.F.T. looks like:

Gratitude | I AM ME BECAUSE...

Today I have my S.H.I.F.T. *together because...*

Today I will keep my S.H.I.F.T. together by...

Gratitude

I am my best self because...

I will push the limits of my S.H.I.F.T. by....

S ——————————————————————

H ——————————————————————

I ——————————————————————

F ——————————————————————

T ——————————————————————

> Your body is perfectly yours. Honor the beauty, radiate your essence, embrace your perfection—**celebrate your inner joy.**
>
> -Dr. Dara

My best S.H.I.F.T. is...

What I need to keep my S.H.I.F.T. together today...

Gratitude — Today I showed up in a big way by...

Getting my S.H.I.F.T. together today looks like...

> "Stop taking yourself so seriously, cause no one else is!"
>
> —Dr. Dara

Month

Sunday	Monday	Tuesday	Wednesday

20 ⎯⎯⎯

Thursday	Friday	Saturday

To-DON'TS

Write down any past stuff that's not welcome in your future.

_____
_____
_____
_____
_____
_____
_____

Ta-DAHS

List what is working, what did work, and what you want more of in your future.

_____
_____
_____
_____
_____
_____
_____

Notes

Spirituality

My monthly spiritual **S.**H.I.F.T. goals

_____
_____
_____
_____
_____
_____
_____
_____
_____
_____
_____
_____
_____
_____
_____
_____

My higher power is defined as…
_____
_____

Spirituality

I am...

Intelligent

Health

My monthly health S.**H**.I.F.T. goals

_____
_____
_____
_____
_____
_____
_____
_____
_____
_____
_____
_____
_____
_____
_____
_____
_____
_____
_____

I nourish my soul with food, exercise, and rest by...
_____
_____

Health

Food · Rest · Exercise

S M T W T F S	nutrition	hours slept	activity	duration
○ ○ ○ ○ ○ ○ ○				
○ ○ ○ ○ ○ ○ ○				
○ ○ ○ ○ ○ ○ ○				
○ ○ ○ ○ ○ ○ ○				
○ ○ ○ ○ ○ ○ ○				
○ ○ ○ ○ ○ ○ ○				
○ ○ ○ ○ ○ ○ ○				
○ ○ ○ ○ ○ ○ ○				
○ ○ ○ ○ ○ ○ ○				
○ ○ ○ ○ ○ ○ ○				
○ ○ ○ ○ ○ ○ ○				
○ ○ ○ ○ ○ ○ ○				
○ ○ ○ ○ ○ ○ ○				
○ ○ ○ ○ ○ ○ ○				
○ ○ ○ ○ ○ ○ ○				

healthy meal ideas: _____
_____

self-care appointments this month: _____
_____

medical appointments this month: _____
_____

Interpersonal

My monthly interpersonal S.H.**I**.F.T. goals

_____
_____
_____
_____
_____
_____
_____
_____
_____
_____
_____
_____
_____
_____
_____

Clubs, groups, or affiliations I would like to have...
_____
_____

Interpersonal

Goals for this month

- Hobbies:
- Vacation plans:
- Time with:
- I feel best when:
- Activities with friends:
- Self-care:
- Self-enrichment:
- Alone time:
- Date night ideas:
- Activities with family:
- Getting out of my comfort zone:

Finance

My monthly finance S.H.I.**F**.T. goals

_____
_____
_____
_____
_____
_____
_____
_____
_____
_____
_____
_____
_____
_____
_____
_____
_____

Money brings me joy because...
_____
_____

Finance

Finance · Budget · Savings

Income

Date	Service	Amount

Debt

Due	Bank	Amount Paid	Balance

Savings

Date	Deposit	Paid Date	Balance

Monthly

Total Income	
Total Budget	
Total Savings	
Total Expenses	

Bills & Expenses

Due	Bank	Amount Paid	Balance

$$ Goals:

Trade

My monthly trade S.H.I.F.**T.** goals

_____
_____
_____
_____
_____
_____
_____
_____
_____
_____
_____
_____
_____
_____
_____
_____
_____
_____
_____
_____

I celebrate my wins by...
_____
_____

Trade

Occupation ∴ Education ∴ Parenting ∴ Tasks

Goals:

Priorities:

Deadlines & Dates

{ SHOULDING ALL OVER YOURSELF? TIRED OF DOING WHAT EVERYONE ELSE THINKS YOU SHOULD? **CHUCK IT IN THE F*CK IT BUCKET** AND LET IT SIMMER DOWN. }

Getting my S.H.I.F.T. together today looks like…

Where my S.H.I.F.T. is *today*...

Gratitude

I am grateful my body can...

Reflections on my S.H.I.F.T.

This is how I S.H.I.F.T.

Sprituality ___

Health ___

Interpersonal ___

Finance ___

Trade ___

> *Progress not perfection.*
>
> —Dr. Dara

Today my best S.H.I.F.T. looks like:

Gratitude

My S.H.I.F.T. is clear because I...

Today I have my S.H.I.F.T. *together because*...

Today I will keep my S.H.I.F.T. together by...

Gratitude

I am my best self when...

I will push the limits of my S.H.I.F.T. by....

S

H

I

F

T

"

The world I see outside
myself is a reflection
of the world I have
shaped within.
The world I experience is
an extension of my mind,
heart, and spirit.

-Dr. Dara

"

My best S.H.I.F.T. is...

What I need to keep my S.H.I.F.T. together today...

Gratitude — I am my best self because…

Getting my S.H.I.F.T. together today looks like...

> Guilt is an a**hole, everyone has one and what comes out of it is sh*t!
>
> —Dr. Dara

Calendar 2023

January
Su	Mo	Tu	We	Th	Fr	Sa
1	2	3	4	5	6	7
8	9	10	11	12	13	14
15	16	17	18	19	20	21
22	23	24	25	26	27	28
29	30	31				

February
Su	Mo	Tu	We	Th	Fr	Sa
			1	2	3	4
5	6	7	8	9	10	11
12	13	14	15	16	17	18
19	20	21	22	23	24	25
26	27	28				

March
Su	Mo	Tu	We	Th	Fr	Sa
			1	2	3	4
5	6	7	8	9	10	11
12	13	14	15	16	17	18
19	20	21	22	23	24	25
26	27	28	29	30	31	

April
Su	Mo	Tu	We	Th	Fr	Sa
						1
2	3	4	5	6	7	8
9	10	11	12	13	14	15
16	17	18	19	20	21	22
23	24	25	26	27	28	29
30						

May
Su	Mo	Tu	We	Th	Fr	Sa
	1	2	3	4	5	6
7	8	9	10	11	12	13
14	15	16	17	18	19	20
21	22	23	24	25	26	27
28	29	30	31			

June
Su	Mo	Tu	We	Th	Fr	Sa
				1	2	3
4	5	6	7	8	9	10
11	12	13	14	15	16	17
18	19	20	21	22	23	24
25	26	27	28	29	30	

July
Su	Mo	Tu	We	Th	Fr	Sa
						1
2	3	4	5	6	7	8
9	10	11	12	13	14	15
16	17	18	19	20	21	22
23	24	25	26	27	28	29
30	31					

August
Su	Mo	Tu	We	Th	Fr	Sa
		1	2	3	4	5
6	7	8	9	10	11	12
13	14	15	16	17	18	19
20	21	22	23	24	25	26
27	28	29	30	31		

September
Su	Mo	Tu	We	Th	Fr	Sa
					1	2
3	4	5	6	7	8	9
10	11	12	13	14	15	16
17	18	19	20	21	22	23
24	25	26	27	28	29	30

October
Su	Mo	Tu	We	Th	Fr	Sa
1	2	3	4	5	6	7
8	9	10	11	12	13	14
15	16	17	18	19	20	21
22	23	24	25	26	27	28
29	30	31				

November
Su	Mo	Tu	We	Th	Fr	Sa
			1	2	3	4
5	6	7	8	9	10	11
12	13	14	15	16	17	18
19	20	21	22	23	24	25
26	27	28	29	30		

December
Su	Mo	Tu	We	Th	Fr	Sa
					1	2
3	4	5	6	7	8	9
10	11	12	13	14	15	16
17	18	19	20	21	22	23
24	25	26	27	28	29	30
31						

Dr. Dara

To-DON'TS

Write down any past stuff that's not welcome in your future.

_____
_____
_____
_____
_____
_____
_____
_____

Ta-DAHS

List what is working, what did work, and what you want more of in your future.

_____
_____
_____
_____
_____
_____
_____
_____

Visions for next year's

S.H.I.F.T.

Spirituality

_____

_____

_____

_____

_____

_____

_____

Health

_____

_____

_____

_____

_____

_____

_____

Interpersonal

Finance

Trade

Notes

> To heal is to notice our strengths and have appreciation for what we do as opposed to shaming ourselves or trying to forgive what we perceive is wrong or broken within us.
>
> -Dr. Dara

Acknowledgments

This may seem like just a fantastic life planner, but it's really a labor of love – a dream created, carried, and birthed with a community of support.

This planner and journal is for you and because of you – my wonderfuls.

Elyah and Nevin – You are my why. You are the reason I shamelessly continue my journey to being the best me I can be for us all.

Randy – Thank you for the endless opportunities to practice grace and to learn how capable I am. A special thanks to you for somehow never tiring of cheering me on through every crazy idea I have. I owe you some new pompoms.

My family – Thank you for the continued love and the fuel to be the woman I am.

My sweetest friends – Thank you for your fire and for never being afraid to give me a taste of my own medicine and tell me to put my big girl panties on and FINISH.

Lesley – my coach, editor, dear friend, and literary goddess – Thank you for seeing my soul, understanding my purpose, and believing that my voice matters. Through you, I found my passion for writing truth and love into this world.

Kim – Thank you for helping me bring my vision to life, vividly and elegantly.

Made in United States
Orlando, FL
15 March 2022